INTRODUCTORY

FOUR STAR

SIGHT READING AND EAR TESTS

DAILY EXERCISES FOR PIANO STUDENTS

BY BORIS BERLIN AND ANDREW MARKOW

Series Editor

SCOTT McBRIDE SMITH

National Library of Canada Cataloguing in Publication Data

Berlin, Boris, 1907-2001
    Four star sight reading and ear tests [music]

ISBN 0-88797-789-8 (Introductory level). —
ISBN 0-88797-791-X (bk. 1). — ISBN 0-88797-793-6 (bk. 2)
ISBN 0-88797-795-2 (bk. 3). — ISBN 0-88797-797-9 (bk. 4)
ISBN 0-88797-799-5 (bk. 5). — ISBN 0-88797-801-0 (bk. 6)
ISBN 0-88797-803-7 (bk. 7). — ISBN 0-88797-805-3 (bk. 8)
ISBN 0-88797-807-X (bk. 9). — ISBN 0-88797-809-6 (bk. 10)

1. Piano — Studies and exercises. 2. Ear training.
3. Sight-reading (Music) I. Markow, Andrew, 1942- II. Title.

MT236.B473 2002   786.2'142'076   C2002-900877-8

ISBN-10: 0-88797-789-8
ISBN-13: 978-0-88797-789-3

PREFACE

The ability to read music at sight at the piano is an important skill for all musicians. As piano students work toward fluency in sight reading, develop aural proficiency, and gain a practical knowledge of theory, they will build a foundation of musicianship that will help them to understand music throughout their lives.

Are some pianists naturally better sight readers than others? Not really. But some recognize patterns on the printed page more readily. Such students use their **visual learning skills**. Other students use their natural **tactile sense** to move around the keyboard quickly. Still others have an innate **aural ability** to hear both melody and harmony with only a glance at the score. Some students may also apply **analytical skills** learned from a study of theory to understand form and content.

The goal of the *Four Star* series is to develop each of these skills and abilities in equal measure. In the process of completing the *Four Star* series, students will improve not only their sight-reading skills but also their proficiency in learning and memorizing music. They will also expand their coordination of eyes, ears, and hands, and their powers of concentration and observation. As a result, *Four Star* students will develop confidence in themselves and in their musical abilities and performance.

Each of the 11 *Four Star* volumes contains daily exercises in sight reading and ear training and builds a foundation for an analytical approach to sight reading music, using examples taken from the standard repertoire. (Some excerpts have been modified by the authors for pedagogical reasons.)

Completion of each *Four Star* book effectively prepares students for the corresponding level of examination systems, including:
- RCM Examinations
- Certificate of Merit (Music Teachers Association of California)
- National Guild of Piano Teachers
- most MTNA curriculums

In order to develop students' reading and overall musical abilities more fully, the authors have chosen to exceed the requirements of most examination systems.

How To Use This Book

The purpose of the *Four Star* series is to provide daily exercises in sight reading and ear training for students to practice at home, as well as tests to be given by the teacher at the lesson. Best results will be obtained through daily student practice, and consistent monitoring and testing at the lesson by the teacher.

SIGHT READING AND RHYTHM

The daily sight-reading and rhythm exercises are intended for students to do by themselves. There are five exercises per week, each including a short piece and clapping rhythm. To indicate a rest while clapping a rhythm, the student should separate their hands and turn their palms upward.
A series of Preliminary Exercises can be found on pp. 4 and 5. It is useful for teachers to review these at the lesson.

EAR TRAINING

Ear-training exercises can be found following the sight-reading and rhythm drills. These, too, are designed to be practiced by the student alone, as assigned by the teacher.

TESTS

Tests are found beginning on p. 26. These are designed to be given by the teacher at the lesson at the conclusion of the corresponding week's work. Supplementary material may be found in the series *Melody Playback/Singback* and *Rhythm Clapback/Singback* by Boris Berlin and Andrew Markow.

PRELIMINARY EXERCISES

Students should familiarize themselves with the notes on the staff in relation to their respective keys on the piano keyboard.

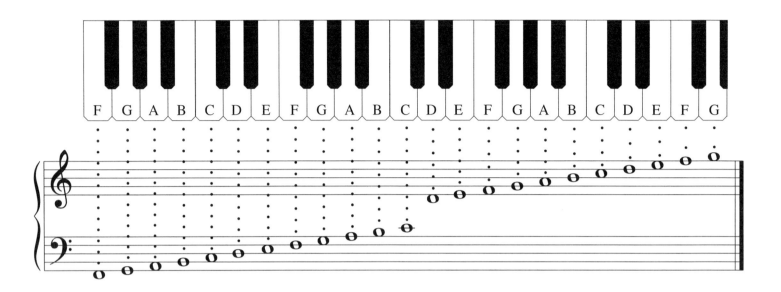

LEARN THE NOTES ON THE LINES

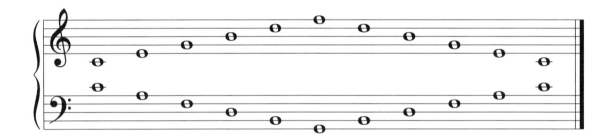

LEARN THE NOTES IN THE SPACES

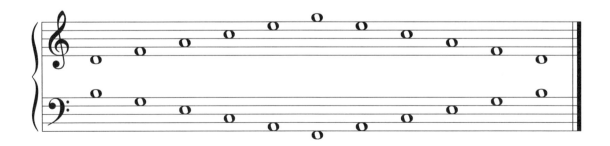

PLAY THE NOTES ON THE LINES

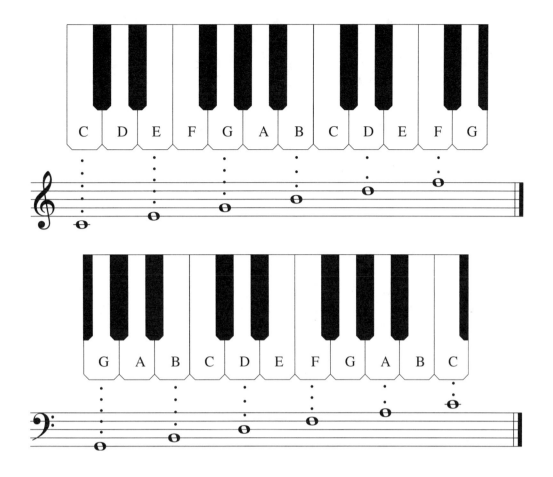

PLAY THE NOTES IN THE SPACES

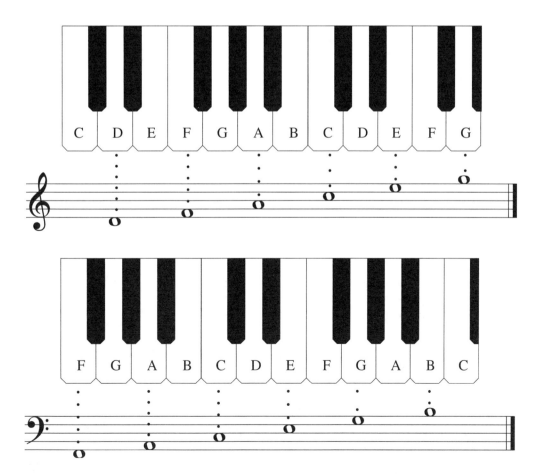

DAILY SIGHT-READING EXERCISES No. 1

Directions to the student: Complete one set of sight-reading exercises at each practice session.

---

1   FIRST DAY _____ (*date*)

1) Name the note and the fingering, then play.

2) Name the first note, then play the melody.

3) Clap or tap the rhythmic pattern while counting the beats.

---

2   SECOND DAY _____ (*date*)

1) Name the note and the fingering, then play.

2) Observe the melodic pattern, then play it.

3) Clap or tap the rhythmic pattern while counting the beats.

---

3   THIRD DAY _____ (*date*)

1) Name the note and the fingering, then play.

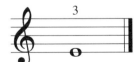

2) Name the first note, then play the melody.

3) Clap or tap the rhythmic pattern while counting the beats.

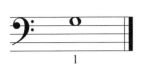 **FOURTH DAY** _____ (*date*)

1) Name the note and the fingering, then play.

2) Observe the melodic pattern, then play it.

3) Clap or tap the rhythmic pattern while counting the beats.

 FIFTH DAY _____ (*date*)

1) Name the note and the fingering, then play.

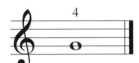 

2) Name the first note, then play the melody.

3) Clap or tap the rhythmic pattern while counting the beats.

DAILY EAR-TRAINING EXERCISES NO. 1

Directions to the student: Complete these ear-training exercises at home.

a) Play this short melody. Then clap, tap, sing, or hum its rhythmic pattern.

b) Play this melodic pattern. Say whether the notes move up or down. Check the correct answer.

The notes move: UP ☐

DOWN ☐

c)

  1) Name the first note.
  2) Mark the number of notes in this melodic pattern.
  3) Mark the direction the notes move (up or down).
  4) Play, first looking at the music, then from memory, listening to the melodic pattern.

  1. The first note is _____ .
  2. This is a __ -note melodic pattern.
  3. The notes move: UP ☐

                DOWN ☐

DAILY SIGHT-READING EXERCISES No. 2

Directions to the student: Complete one set of sight-reading exercises at each practice session.

1 FIRST DAY _____ (*date*)

1) Name the note and the fingering, then play.

2) Name the first note, then play the melody.

3) Clap or tap the rhythmic pattern while counting the beats.

2 SECOND DAY _____ (*date*)

1) Name the note and the fingering, then play.

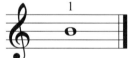

2) Observe the melodic pattern, then play it.

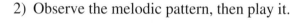

3) Clap or tap the rhythmic pattern while counting the beats.

3 THIRD DAY _____ (*date*)

1) Name the note and the fingering, then play.

2) Name the first note, then play the melody.

3) Clap or tap the rhythmic pattern while counting the beats.

4 FOURTH DAY _____ (*date*)

1) Name the note and the fingering, then play.

2) Observe the melodic pattern, then play it.

3) Clap or tap the rhythmic pattern while counting the beats.

---

5 FIFTH DAY _____ (*date*)

1) Name the note and the fingering, then play.

2) Name the first note, then play the melody.

3) Clap or tap the rhythmic pattern while counting the beats.

DAILY EAR-TRAINING EXERCISES No. 2

Directions to the student: Complete these ear-training exercises at home.

---

a)   Play this short melody. Then clap, tap, sing, or hum its rhythmic pattern.

b)   Play this melodic pattern. Say whether the notes move up or down. Check the correct answer.

The notes move: UP   ☐

DOWN   ☐

c)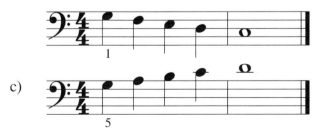

1) Name the first note.
2) Mark the number of notes in this melodic pattern.
3) Mark the direction the notes move (up or down).
4) Play, first looking at the music, then from memory, listening to the melodic pattern.

1. The first note is _____ .
2. This is a ___ -note melodic pattern.
3. The notes move: UP   ☐

DOWN   ☐

DAILY SIGHT-READING EXERCISES NO. 3

Directions to the student: Complete one set of sight-reading exercises at each practice session.

1 FIRST DAY _____ (date)

1) Name the note and the fingering, then play.

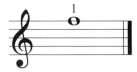 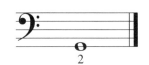

2) Name the first note, then play the melody.

3) Clap or tap the rhythmic pattern while counting the beats.

2 SECOND DAY _____ (date)

1) Name the note and the fingering, then play.

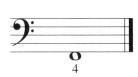 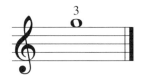

2) Observe the melodic pattern, then play it.

3) Clap or tap the rhythmic pattern while counting the beats.

3 THIRD DAY _____ (date)

1) Name the notes and the fingering, then play.

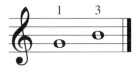 

2) Name the first note, then play the melody.

3) Clap or tap the rhythmic pattern while counting the beats.

4 FOURTH DAY _____ (*date*)

1) Name the notes and the fingering, then play.

 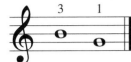

2) Observe the melodic pattern, then play it.

3) Clap or tap the rhythmic pattern while counting the beats.

---

5 FIFTH DAY _____ (*date*)

1) Name the notes and the fingering, then play.

 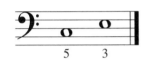

2) Name the first note, then play the melody.

3) Clap or tap the rhythmic pattern while counting the beats.

DAILY EAR-TRAINING EXERCISES NO. 3

Directions to the student: Complete these ear-training exercises at home.

a) Play this short melody. Then clap, tap, sing, or hum its rhythmic pattern.

b) Play this melodic pattern. Say whether the notes move up or down. Check the correct answer.

The notes move: UP ☐

DOWN ☐

c)

1) Name the first note.
2) Mark the number of notes in this melodic pattern.
3) Mark the direction the notes move (up or down).
4) Play, first looking at the music, then from memory, listening to the melodic pattern.

1. The first note is _____ .
2. This is a __ -note melodic pattern.
3. The notes move: UP ☐

DOWN ☐

DAILY SIGHT-READING EXERCISES NO. 4

Directions to the student: Complete one set of sight-reading exercises at each practice session.

1   FIRST DAY _____ (*date*)

1) Name the notes and the fingering, then play.
2) Name the first note, then play the melody.

3) Clap or tap the rhythmic pattern while counting the beats.

2   SECOND DAY _____ (*date*)

1) Name the notes and the fingering, then play.
2) Observe the melodic pattern, then play it.

 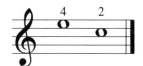 

3) Clap or tap the rhythmic pattern while counting the beats.

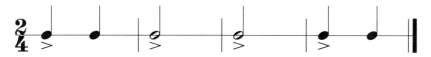

3   THIRD DAY _____ (*date*)

1) Name the notes and the fingering, then play.
2) Name the first note, then play the melody.

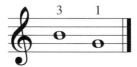  

3) Clap or tap the rhythmic pattern while counting the beats.

4 FOURTH DAY _____ (date)

1) Name the notes and the fingering, then play.

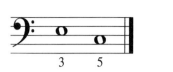 

2) Observe the melodic pattern, then play it.

3) Clap or tap the rhythmic pattern while counting the beats.

5 FIFTH DAY _____ (date)

1) Name the notes and the fingering, then play.

 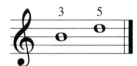 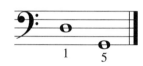

2) Name the first note, then play the melody.

3) Clap or tap the rhythmic pattern while counting the beats.

DAILY EAR-TRAINING EXERCISES NO. 4

Directions to the student: Complete these ear-training exercises at home.

a) Play this short melody. Then clap, tap, sing, or hum its rhythmic pattern.

b) Play this melodic pattern. Say whether the notes move up or down. Check the correct answer.

The notes move: UP ☐

DOWN ☐

c)

1) Name the first note.
2) Mark the number of notes in this melodic pattern.
3) Mark the direction the notes move (up or down).
4) Play, first looking at the music, then from memory, listening to the melodic pattern.

1. The first note is _____ .
2. This is a __ -note melodic pattern.
3. The notes move: UP ☐

DOWN ☐

DAILY SIGHT-READING EXERCISES No. 5

Directions to the student: Complete one set of sight-reading exercises at each practice session.

---

1   FIRST DAY _____ (date)

1) Name the notes and the fingering, then play.

2) Name the first note, then play the melody.

3) Clap or tap the rhythmic pattern while counting the beats.

---

2   SECOND DAY _____ (date)

1) Name the notes and the fingering, then play.

2) Observe the melodic pattern, then play it.

3) Clap or tap the rhythmic pattern while counting the beats.

---

3   THIRD DAY _____ (date)

1) Name the notes and the fingering, then play.

2) Name the first note, then play the melody.

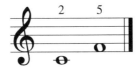

3) Clap or tap the rhythmic pattern while counting the beats.

4 FOURTH DAY _____ (*date*)

1) Name the notes and the fingering, then play.

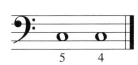 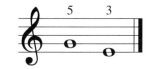

2) Observe the melodic pattern, then play it.

3) Clap or tap the rhythmic pattern while counting the beats.

---

5 FIFTH DAY _____ (*date*)

1) Name the notes and the fingering, then play.

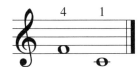 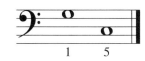

2) Name the first note, then play the melody.

3) Clap or tap the rhythmic pattern while counting the beats.

DAILY EAR-TRAINING EXERCISES NO. 5

Directions to the student: Complete these ear-training exercises at home.

a) Play this short melody. Then clap, tap, sing, or hum its rhythmic pattern.

b) Play this melodic pattern. Say whether the notes move up or down. Check the correct answer.

The notes move: UP ☐

DOWN ☐

c)

1) Name the first note.
2) Mark the number of notes in this melodic pattern.
3) Mark the direction the notes move (up or down).
4) Play, first looking at the music, then from memory, listening to the melodic pattern.

1. The first note is _____ .
2. This is a __ -note melodic pattern.
3. The notes move: UP ☐

DOWN ☐

DAILY SIGHT-READING EXERCISES NO. 6

Directions to the student: Complete one set of sight-reading exercises at each practice session.

1   FIRST DAY _____ (*date*)

1) Name the notes and the fingering, then play.   2) Name the first note, then play the melody.

3) Clap or tap the rhythmic pattern while counting the beats.

---

2   SECOND DAY _____ (*date*)

1) Name the notes and the fingering, then play.   2) Observe the melodic pattern, then play it.

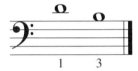  

3) Clap or tap the rhythmic pattern while counting the beats.

---

3   THIRD DAY _____ (*date*)

1) Name the notes and the fingering, then play.   2) Name the first note, then play the melody.

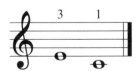  

3) Clap or tap the rhythmic pattern while counting the beats.

4 FOURTH DAY _____ (*date*)

1) Name the notes and the fingering, then play.

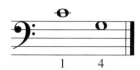 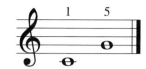

2) Observe the melodic pattern, then play it.

3) Clap or tap the rhythmic pattern while counting the beats.

5 FIFTH DAY _____ (*date*)

1) Name the notes and the fingering, then play.

2) Name the first note, then play the melody.

3) Clap or tap the rhythmic pattern while counting the beats.

DAILY EAR-TRAINING EXERCISES No. 6

Directions to the student: Complete these ear-training exercises at home.

a)   Play this short melody. Then clap, tap, sing, or hum its rhythmic pattern.

b)   Play this melodic pattern. Say whether the notes move up or down. Check the correct answer.

The notes move: UP   ☐

DOWN   ☐

c)

1) Name the first note.
2) Mark the number of notes in this melodic pattern.
3) Mark the direction the notes move (up or down).
4) Play, first looking at the music, then from memory, listening to the melodic pattern.

1. The first note is _____ .
2. This is a __ -note melodic pattern.
3. The notes move: UP   ☐

DOWN   ☐

DAILY SIGHT-READING EXERCISES No. 7

Directions to the student: Complete one set of sight-reading exercises at each practice session.

1   FIRST DAY _____ (*date*)

1) Name the notes and the fingering, then play.

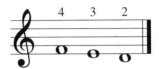 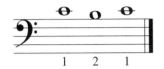

2) Name the first note in each hand, then play.

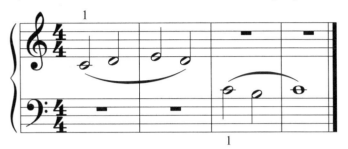

3) Clap or tap the rhythmic pattern while counting the beats.

2   SECOND DAY _____ (*date*)

1) Name the notes and the fingering, then play.

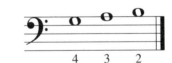 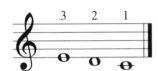

2) Observe the melodic patterns, then play.

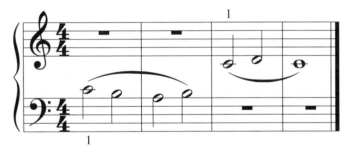

3) Clap or tap the rhythmic pattern while counting the beats.

3   THIRD DAY _____ (*date*)

1) Name the notes and the fingering, then play.

 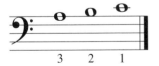

2) Name the last note in each hand, then play.

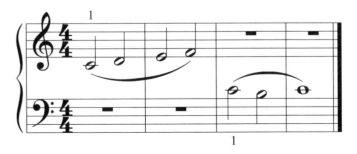

3) Clap or tap the rhythmic pattern while counting the beats.

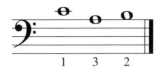 FOURTH DAY _____ (*date*)

1) Name the notes and the fingering, then play.

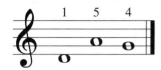

2) Observe the melodic patterns, then play.

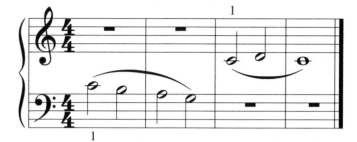

3) Clap or tap the rhythmic pattern while counting the beats.

 FIFTH DAY _____ (*date*)

1) Name the notes and the fingering, then play.

 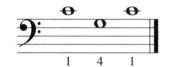

2) Name the last note in each hand, then play.

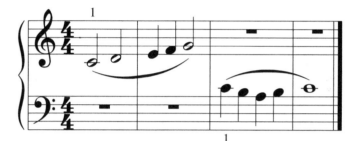

3) Clap or tap the rhythmic pattern while counting the beats.

DAILY EAR-TRAINING EXERCISES No. 7

Directions to the student: Complete these ear-training exercises at home.

a) Play this short melody. Then clap, tap, sing, or hum its rhythmic pattern.

b) Play this melodic pattern. Say whether the notes move up or down. Check the correct answer.

The notes move: UP   ☐

                DOWN   ☐

c)

   1) Name the first note.

   2) Mark the number of notes in this melodic pattern.

   3) Mark the direction the notes move (up or down).

   4) Play, first looking at the music, then from memory, listening to the melodic pattern.

   1. The first note is _____ .

   2. This is a __ -note melodic pattern.

   3. The notes move: UP   ☐

                 DOWN   ☐

Daily Sight-Reading Exercises No. 8

Directions to the student: Complete one set of sight-reading exercises at each practice session.

1   FIRST DAY _____ (*date*)

1) Name the notes and the fingering, then play.

2) Name the first note in each hand, then play.

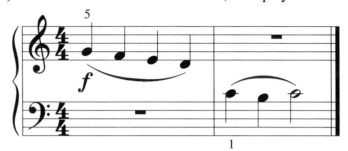

3) Clap or tap the rhythmic pattern while counting the beats.

2   SECOND DAY _____ (*date*)

1) Name the notes and the fingering, then play.

 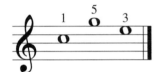

2) Observe the melodic patterns, then play.

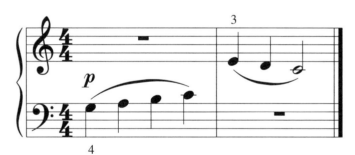

3) Clap or tap the rhythmic pattern while counting the beats.

3   THIRD DAY _____ (*date*)

1) Name the notes and the fingering, then play.

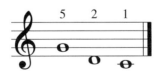 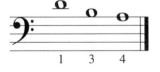

2) Name the last note in each hand, then play.

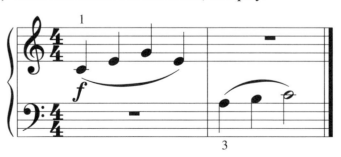

3) Clap or tap the rhythmic pattern while counting the beats.

4 **FOURTH DAY** _____ (*date*)

1) Name the notes and the fingering, then play.

 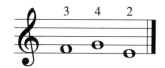

2) Observe the melodic patterns, then play.

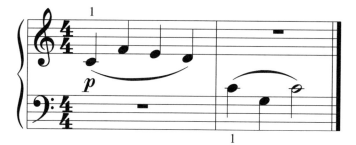

3) Clap or tap the rhythmic pattern while counting the beats.

5 **FIFTH DAY** _____ (*date*)

1) Name the notes and the fingering, then play.

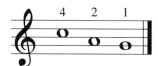 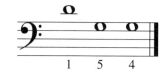

2) Name the first note in each hand, then play.

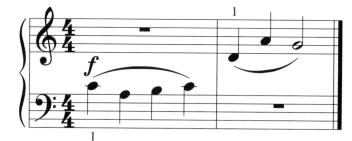

3) Clap or tap the rhythmic pattern while counting the beats.

DAILY EAR-TRAINING EXERCISES No. 8

Directions to the student: Complete these ear-training exercises at home.

a)   Play this short melody. Then clap, tap, sing, or hum its rhythmic pattern.

b)   Play this melodic pattern. Say whether the notes move up or down. Check the correct answer.

The notes move: UP   ☐

DOWN   ☐

c)

1) Name the first note.
2) Mark the number of notes in this melodic pattern.
3) Mark the direction the notes move (up or down).
4) Play, first looking at the music, then from memory, listening to the melodic pattern.

1. The first note is _____ .
2. This is a __ -note melodic pattern.
3. The notes move: UP   ☐

DOWN   ☐

DAILY SIGHT-READING EXERCISES No. 9

Directions to the student: Complete one set of sight-reading exercises at each practice session.

1 FIRST DAY _____ (*date*)

1) Name the notes and the fingering, then play.

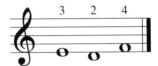 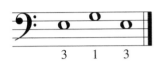

2) Name the first note in each hand, then play.

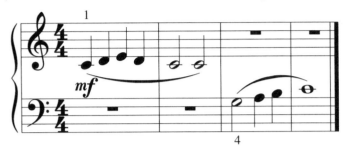

3) Clap or tap the rhythmic pattern while counting the beats.

2 SECOND DAY _____ (*date*)

1) Name the notes and the fingering, then play.

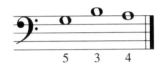 

2) Observe the melodic patterns, then play.

3) Clap or tap the rhythmic pattern while counting the beats.

3 THIRD DAY _____ (*date*)

1) Name the notes and the fingering, then play.

 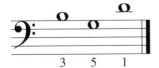

2) Name the last note in each hand, then play.

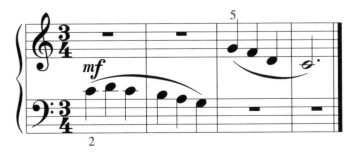

3) Clap or tap the rhythmic pattern while counting the beats.

23

4 FOURTH DAY _____ (date)

1) Name the notes and the fingering, then play.

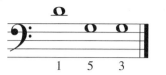 

2) Observe the melodic patterns, then play.

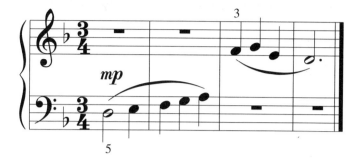

3) Clap or tap the rhythmic pattern while counting the beats.

5 FIFTH DAY _____ (date)

1) Name the notes and the fingering, then play.

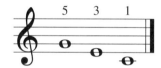 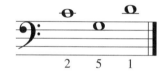

2) Name the first note in each hand, then play.

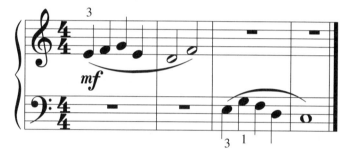

3) Clap or tap the rhythmic pattern while counting the beats.

DAILY EAR-TRAINING EXERCISES No. 9

Directions to the student: Complete these ear-training exercises at home.

a) Play this short melody. Then clap, tap, sing, or hum its rhythmic pattern.

b) Play this melodic pattern. Say whether the notes move up or down. Check the correct answer.

The notes move: UP ☐
DOWN ☐

c)

1) Name the first note.
2) Mark the number of notes in this melodic pattern.
3) Mark the direction the notes move (up or down).
4) Play, first looking at the music, then from memory, listening to the melodic pattern.

1. The first note is _____ .
2. This is a __ -note melodic pattern.
3. The notes move: UP ☐
DOWN ☐

DAILY SIGHT-READING EXERCISES No. 10

Directions to the student: Complete one set of sight-reading exercises at each practice session.

1   FIRST DAY _____ (*date*)

1) Name the notes and the fingering, then play.

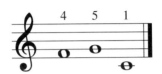 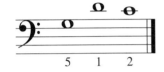

2) Name the last note in each hand, then play.

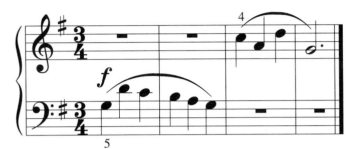

3) Clap or tap the rhythmic pattern while counting the beats.

2   SECOND DAY _____ (*date*)

1) Name the notes and the fingering, then play.

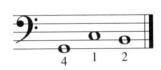 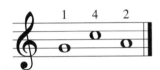

2) Observe the melodic patterns, then play.

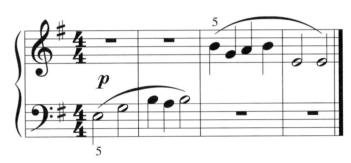

3) Clap or tap the rhythmic pattern while counting the beats.

3   THIRD DAY _____ (*date*)

1) Name the notes and the fingering, then play.

 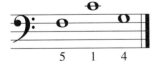

2) Name the first note in each hand, then play.

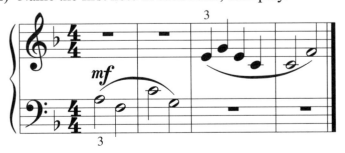

3) Clap or tap the rhythmic pattern while counting the beats.

4 FOURTH DAY _____ (date)

1) Name the notes and the fingering, then play.

2) Observe the melodic patterns, then play.

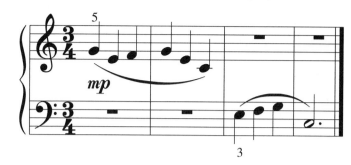

3) Clap or tap the rhythmic pattern while counting the beats.

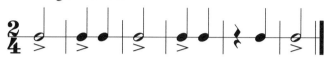

5 FIFTH DAY _____ (date)

1) Name the notes and the fingering, then play.

2) Name the last note in each hand, then play.

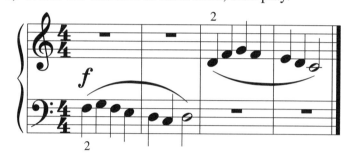

3) Clap or tap the rhythmic pattern while counting the beats.

DAILY EAR-TRAINING EXERCISES No. 10

Directions to the student: Complete these ear-training exercises at home.

---

a)   Play this short melody. Then clap, tap, sing, or hum its rhythmic pattern.

b)   Play this melodic pattern. Say whether the notes move up or down. Check the correct answer.

The notes move: UP   ☐

DOWN   ☐

c)

1) Name the first note.
2) Mark the number of notes in this melodic pattern.
3) Mark the direction the notes move (up or down).
4) Play, first looking at the music, then from memory, listening to the melodic pattern.

1. The first note is _____ .
2. This is a ___ -note melodic pattern.
3. The notes move: UP   ☐

DOWN   ☐

FOUR STAR TESTS
GIVEN BY THE TEACHER AT THE LESSON

★ FOUR STAR TEST NO. 1 ★

SIGHT-READING TEST

Teacher's grading

Play with the given fingering.

Name the first note, the number of notes and their direction (moving up or down), then play.

Clap or tap the rhythmic pattern.

EAR TEST

All the material for the following Ear Tests can be found on pp. 31 and 32.

1) The teacher selects any one of the short melodies from p. 31 and plays it twice for the student. The student then claps, taps, sings, or hums the rhythm.

2) The teacher selects any one of the simple melodies from p. 32 and plays it twice for the student. The student then says whether the notes move up or down.

3) The teacher selects any one of the patterns from p. 32, plays it twice, and then shows the student the beginning note. The student then plays the melodic pattern back on the piano.

★ FOUR STAR TEST NO. 2 ★

SIGHT-READING TEST

Teacher's grading

Play with the given fingering.

Name the first note, the number of notes and their direction (moving up or down), then play.

Clap or tap the rhythmic pattern.

EAR TEST

All the material for the following Ear Tests can be found on pp. 31 and 32.

1) The teacher selects any one of the short melodies from p. 31 and plays it twice for the student. The student then claps, taps, sings, or hums the rhythm.

2) The teacher selects any one of the simple melodies from p. 32 and plays it twice for the student. The student then says whether the notes move up or down.

3) The teacher selects any one of the patterns from p. 32, plays it twice, and then shows the student the beginning note. The student then plays the melodic pattern back on the piano.

★ Four Star Test No. 3 ★

SIGHT-READING TEST

Teacher's grading

Play with the given fingering.

Name the first note, the number of notes and their direction (moving up or down), then play.

Clap or tap the rhythmic pattern.

EAR TEST

All the material for the following Ear Tests can be found on pp. 31 and 32.

1) The teacher selects any one of the short melodies from p. 31 and plays it twice for the student. The student then claps, taps, sings, or hums the rhythm.

2) The teacher selects any one of the simple melodies from p. 32 and plays it twice for the student. The student then says whether the notes move up or down.

3) The teacher selects any one of the patterns from p. 32, plays it twice, and then shows the student the beginning note. The student then plays the melodic pattern back on the piano.

★ Four Star Test No. 4 ★

SIGHT-READING TEST

Teacher's grading

Play with the given fingering.

Name the first note, the number of notes and their direction (moving up or down), then play.

Clap or tap the rhythmic pattern.

EAR TEST

All the material for the following Ear Tests can be found on pp. 31 and 32.

1) The teacher selects any one of the short melodies from p. 31 and plays it twice for the student. The student then claps, taps, sings, or hums the rhythm.

2) The teacher selects any one of the simple melodies from p. 32 and plays it twice for the student. The student then says whether the notes move up or down.

3) The teacher selects any one of the patterns from p. 32, plays it twice, and then shows the student the beginning note. The student then plays the melodic pattern back on the piano.

★ FOUR STAR TEST NO. 5 ★

SIGHT-READING TEST

Teacher's grading

Play with the given fingering.

Name the first note, the number of notes and their direction (moving up or down), then play.

Clap or tap the rhythmic pattern.

EAR TEST

All the material for the following Ear Tests can be found on pp. 31 and 32.

1) The teacher selects any one of the short melodies from p. 31 and plays it twice for the student. The student then claps, taps, sings, or hums the rhythm.

2) The teacher selects any one of the simple melodies from p. 32 and plays it twice for the student. The student then says whether the notes move up or down.

3) The teacher selects any one of the patterns from p. 32, plays it twice, and then shows the student the beginning note. The student then plays the melodic pattern back on the piano.

★ FOUR STAR TEST NO. 6 ★

SIGHT-READING TEST

Teacher's grading

Play with the given fingering.

Name the first note, the number of notes and their direction (moving up or down), then play.

Clap or tap the rhythmic pattern.

EAR TEST

All the material for the following Ear Tests can be found on pp. 31 and 32.

1) The teacher selects any one of the short melodies from p. 31 and plays it twice for the student. The student then claps, taps, sings, or hums the rhythm.

2) The teacher selects any one of the simple melodies from p. 32 and plays it twice for the student. The student then says whether the notes move up or down.

3) The teacher selects any one of the patterns from p. 32, plays it twice, and then shows the student the beginning note. The student then plays the melodic pattern back on the piano.

★ FOUR STAR TEST NO. 7 ★

SIGHT-READING TEST

Teacher's grading

Play with the given fingering.

Name the first note, the number of notes and their direction (moving up or down), then play.

Clap or tap the rhythmic pattern.

EAR TEST

All the material for the following Ear Tests can be found on pp. 31 and 32.

1) The teacher selects any one of the short melodies from p. 31 and plays it twice for the student. The student then claps, taps, sings, or hums the rhythm.

2) The teacher selects any one of the simple melodies from p. 32 and plays it twice for the student. The student then says whether the notes move up or down.

3) The teacher selects any one of the patterns from p. 32, plays it twice, and then shows the student the beginning note. The student then plays the melodic pattern back on the piano.

★ FOUR STAR TEST NO. 8 ★

SIGHT-READING TEST

Teacher's grading

Play with the given fingering.

Name the first note, the number of notes and their direction (moving up or down), then play.

Clap or tap the rhythmic pattern.

EAR TEST

All the material for the following Ear Tests can be found on pp. 31 and 32.

1) The teacher selects any one of the short melodies from p. 31 and plays it twice for the student. The student then claps, taps, sings, or hums the rhythm.

2) The teacher selects any one of the simple melodies from p. 32 and plays it twice for the student. The student then says whether the notes move up or down.

3) The teacher selects any one of the patterns from p. 32, plays it twice, and then shows the student the beginning note. The student then plays the melodic pattern back on the piano.

★ FOUR STAR TEST NO. 9 ★

SIGHT-READING TEST

Teacher's grading

Play with the given fingering.

Name the first note, the number of notes and their direction (moving up or down), then play.

Clap or tap the rhythmic pattern.

EAR TEST

All the material for the following Ear Tests can be found on pp. 31 and 32.

1) The teacher selects any one of the short melodies from p. 31 and plays it twice for the student. The student then claps, taps, sings, or hums the rhythm.

2) The teacher selects any one of the simple melodies from p. 32 and plays it twice for the student. The student then says whether the notes move up or down.

3) The teacher selects any one of the patterns from p. 32, plays it twice, and then shows the student the beginning note. The student then plays the melodic pattern back on the piano.

★ FOUR STAR TEST NO. 10 ★

SIGHT-READING TEST

Teacher's grading

Play with the given fingering.

Name the first note, the number of notes and their direction (moving up or down), then play.

Clap or tap the rhythmic pattern.

EAR TEST

All the material for the following Ear Tests can be found on pp. 31 and 32.

1) The teacher selects any one of the short melodies from p. 31 and plays it twice for the student. The student then claps, taps, sings, or hums the rhythm.

2) The teacher selects any one of the simple melodies from p. 32 and plays it twice for the student. The student then says whether the notes move up or down.

3) The teacher selects any one of the patterns from p. 32, plays it twice, and then shows the student the beginning note. The student then plays the melodic pattern back on the piano.

EAR TESTS
GIVEN BY THE TEACHER AT THE LESSON

During these tests, the student must not see the keyboard or look at the music.

1) The teacher selects one of the following short melodies and plays it TWICE.
   The student then claps, taps, sings, or hums the rhythm of the short melody from memory.

32

2) The teacher plays any one of these simple melodies TWICE.
The student then says whether the notes of the melody move up or down.

3) The teacher chooses any one of these short melodic patterns and:
   a) plays the melodic pattern TWICE;
   b) shows the student the beginning note.

The student then plays the melodic pattern back on the piano.